PYTHAGORAS
and the Ratios

A Math Adventure

Julie Ellis

Illustrated by Phyllis Hornung Peacock

Charlesbridge

To Joshua, a curious boy who likes math and
finding out how things work—J. E.
For Lauren and Lindsay Hoffman and Amanda
and Ashley Hornung—P. H. P.

Text copyright © 2010 by Julie Ellis
Illustrations copyright © 2010 by Phyllis Hornung Peacock

Published by Charlesbridge
85 Main Street
Watertown, MA 02472
(617) 926-0329
www.charlesbridge.com

Library of Congress Cataloging-in-Publication Data
Ellis, Julie, 1961–
    Pythagoras and the ratios / Julie Ellis; illustrated by Phyllis Hornung Peacock.
        p. cm.
    ISBN 978-1-57091-775-2 (reinforced for library use)
    ISBN 978-1-57091-776-9 (softcover)
    ISBN 978-1-60734-189-5 (ebook pdf)
1. Pythagorean theorem—Juvenile literature. 2. Ratio and proportion—
Juvenile literature. I. Peacock, Phyllis Hornung, ill. II. Title.
QA460.P8E378 2010
516.22—dc22   2009004306

Printed in Korea
(hc) 10 9 8 7 6 5 4 3 2 1
(sc) 10 9 8 7 6 5 4

Illustrations done in acrylic and colored pencil on Fabriano Artistico
    300-pound cold-press watercolor paper
Display type and text type set in Sierra and Flare821 BT
Color separations by Chroma Graphics, Singapore
Printed by Sung In Printing in Gunpo-Si, Kyonggi-Do, Korea
Production supervision by Brian G. Walker
Designed by Martha MacLeod Sikkema

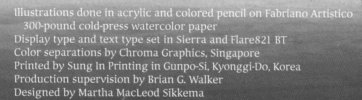

Long ago in ancient Greece, there lived a curious boy named Pythagoras. He liked finding out how things worked, which sometimes caused him to forget to finish his chores.

One day Pythagoras had just finished proving that rocks cannot float when he heard a deep and horrible howling sound.

"Zeus's beard!" he yelled. "What is that?"

He followed the sound to the top of a hill overlooking the harbor.

"Octavius," said Pythagoras to his cousin, "were you making that awful noise?"

"Unfortunately, yes," Octavius said, nodding. "I made these new pipes for the music contest. They sound so bad that my parents sent me outside to practice. If I can't figure out what's wrong, I won't be able to compete in the contest."

"Let me try," Pythagoras suggested. He played the same awful sounds. "By Apollo's hammer, that is terrible!"

"Well," Octavius said, "at least it isn't me—it's definitely the pipes."

"Hmm . . . I wonder how they are different from mine." Pythagoras said to Octavius. "I'll get my pipes and a measuring cord. Can you get a stylus and a clay tablet?"

Pythagoras measured the length and width of each pipe. Octavius used the stylus to scratch the measurements into the clay tablet.

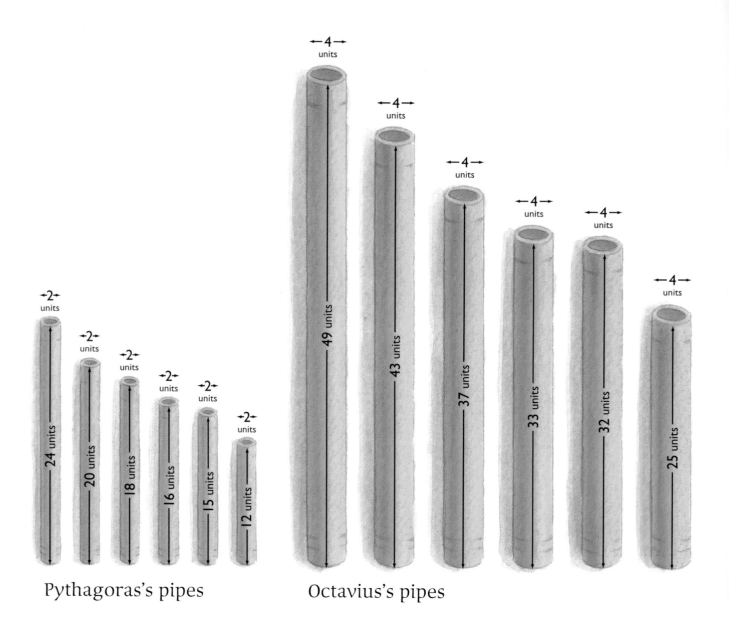

Pythagoras's pipes   Octavius's pipes

"Look at how the length of the shortest of my pipes compares to the longest," Pythagoras said. "Octavius, write the length of each of my pipes above the length of the shortest."

Octavius wrote 24 over 12, then 20 over 12, and so on, to compare the other five pipes to the shortest one.

"We can simplify these numbers," Pythagoras said, "if we divide both the top and bottom numbers by the greatest common factor. For 24 over 12, I can divide both by 12."

For each pair Pythagoras figured out the biggest number that could go into the top and bottom numbers.

Pipe	Relationship to Smallest Pipe	Simplifying by the Greatest Common Factor	Simplified Relationship
Pipe 6	$\dfrac{24}{12}$	$\dfrac{(24 \div 12)}{(12 \div 12)}$	2 to 1
Pipe 5	$\dfrac{20}{12}$	$\dfrac{(20 \div 4)}{(12 \div 4)}$	5 to 3
Pipe 4	$\dfrac{18}{12}$	$\dfrac{(18 \div 6)}{(12 \div 6)}$	3 to 2
Pipe 3	$\dfrac{16}{12}$	$\dfrac{(16 \div 4)}{(12 \div 4)}$	4 to 3
Pipe 2	$\dfrac{15}{12}$	$\dfrac{(15 \div 3)}{(12 \div 3)}$	5 to 4
Pipe 1	$\dfrac{12}{12}$	$\dfrac{(12 \div 12)}{(12 \div 12)}$	1 to 1

"I wonder if the relationship among my pipes is what makes them sound good together." Pythagoras compared the two sets of pipes. "Each of your pipes is exactly twice as wide as mine," he said, "but they are more than twice as long.

"If the relationship that we've discovered works for my pipes, maybe it will work for yours, too. We can't change the width of your pipes, but we can change the length. Let's cut your pipes so that each one is exactly twice as long as mine."

"Cut them!" Octavius cried. "What if they sound worse?"

"Believe me," Pythagoras said, "nothing could sound worse."

Pythagoras cut Octavius's pipes. Then Octavius
played them.

"Now your pipes sound like mine," Pythagoras said,
"only yours still sound deep while mine sound lighter.
I'll bet that's because your pipes are wider. I wonder
what would happen if we played at the same time."

"No one plays pipes together," answered Octavius. "It sounds horrible."

Pythagoras shrugged. "It couldn't be worse than how you sounded earlier."

Octavius agreed. "Do you know 'Ode to Apollo'?"

Pythagoras nodded, and they began to play. The sounds were in tune.

"It worked," Pythagoras said excitedly. "The lengths of the pipes control how high or low the sound is."

"Here come Amara and Reyna," Octavius said. "Let's hear what they think."

"That sounded excellent, but we've come to warn you, Pythagoras. You're in trouble," his cousin Amara said.

"What have I done now?" Pythagoras asked.

"Nothing," Reyna said. "*That's* the trouble. You were supposed to help your father gather olives today."

"Oh, no, I forgot all about it!" Pythagoras cried, and he ran toward the olive grove.

"Father," Pythagoras gasped, "I'm sorry I forgot about the olives, but I made an amazing discovery. I know how to tune pipes!"

"You need to tune in to your responsibilities," his father replied sternly. "Now fill this pannier with olives and then come home."

Pythagoras had just started to work when Amara and Reyna found him.

"We tried to play our lyres together," Amara said, "but they sounded awful."

"Can you fix our lyres like you did Octavius's pipes?" Reyna asked. "We want to prove to our brothers that we are good enough to enter the music contest, too."

"Help me pick up these olives," Pythagoras said, "and then I'll try to figure out your lyres."

When the pannier was full, Pythagoras led the donkey home. Then Amara and Reyna showed their lyres to Pythagoras.

"It may be that the relationship between each lyre string has to be the same as the relationship between the length of my pipes," Pythagoras said. "We just have to figure out what that relationship is."

"But lyre strings are all the same length and thickness," Reyna said.

"Yes," Pythagoras agreed, "so something else about the strings has to change."

Just then his mother walked in.

"Pythagoras," she said, "the mason is coming tomorrow to rebuild our wall. Please move the rocks out of the way and sort them into piles by size this afternoon."

Pythagoras told the girls he'd see them later and went to work sorting the rocks. Suddenly he had an idea.

"Rocks are different weights," he said excitedly. "Maybe putting different weights on the strings would have the same effect as changing the lengths of the pipes."

Pythagoras weighed rocks until he found some with a 2 to 1 relationship to use for the first and last strings. Then he found four others with the same relationships as the middle pipes.

I can't wait to test my idea, Pythagoras thought as he went in for dinner, forgetting about moving the rest of the rocks.

The next morning Pythagoras went looking for Reyna and Amara. They had already left for the marketplace.

He was sure they wouldn't mind, so he went inside and got their lyres. He untied the strings on Amara's lyre and tied a rock to each one. Then he plucked each string and played his pipe. The notes matched!

Pythagoras was working on Reyna's lyre when the girls returned.

"What are you doing?" Amara cried.

"I figured out how to make the lyre sounds match my pipes," Pythagoras answered. "The relationship between the weights of these rocks is the same as the relationship between the lengths of my pipes."

"How can I play a lyre with rocks swinging back and forth, hitting me?" Amara complained.

19

"We need the rocks in order to make the right amount of pull on each string. You'll just have to be careful when you play so the rocks don't hit you," Pythagoras said.

"I think it's interesting," Reyna said. "We'll be the only girls with rocks on our lyres."

The girls tested their lyres by playing a song. Pythagoras joined in on his pipes.

"That was beautiful," Reyna said, smiling.

"I've never heard anything like it," Amara agreed.

"Let's find Octavius," Reyna said. "Then all four of us can play together at the contest."

"The judges might not let us," Pythagoras said.

"It'll be a secret!" Amara burst out. "I'll find Octavius and ask him to join us tomorrow to practice before the contest."

"Great!" Pythagoras exclaimed. "I can't wait."

When Pythagoras got home that evening, his father was waiting for him.

"Today the mason went home because the rocks were not moved out of his way," his father said. "Your mother asked you to do that yesterday."

Pythagoras tried to explain. "When I felt the weight of the rocks, I got a great idea. It was the solution I needed, and now when we play in the contest . . ."

"Stop right there, Pythagoras, and take note of what I say. I know the contest is important, but so are your responsibilities. You may not go anywhere until you move all those rocks."

"Father, please!" Pythagoras pleaded. "There's not enough time to move them before the contest."

"It's the only way you'll remember to finish your chores the next time you're distracted by a new idea," his father replied.

Early the next morning Octavius found Pythagoras moving rocks.

"Amara told me the plan," said Octavius.

"I can't go." Pythagoras explained what had happened. "It'll take me too long to move all these rocks."

"I'll help you," Octavius said. "Look, here come Thanos and Ionius. They might help us, too."

"We've come to tell you that our sisters won't be joining you," announced Thanos.

"We don't want them to embarrass the family by trying to play their lyres together," Ionius added.

"They won't," Pythagoras answered. "Just listen to this."

He and Octavius played "Ode to Apollo."

"That actually sounded good," Ionius exclaimed.

"I liked it, too," Thanos added. "I'm sorry we started on the wrong note. Can we join your group?"

"I would have to fix your pipes," Pythagoras said. "But I can't do that until I move all these rocks."

"We'll help you," Thanos said.

"We'll get Amara and Reyna to help, too," Ionius added.

All five cousins pitched in to help, and soon the rocks were sorted. Then Pythagoras fixed Thanos's and Ionius's pipes the same way he had fixed Octavius's. When they were finished, they rushed to the amphitheater.

All the way Pythagoras kept saying what great cousins they were and thanking them. He was looking over his shoulder when it happened. Pythagoras tripped. His pipes were in pieces on the ground.

"This is awful," Amara said, looking at the broken pieces.

"Well, *I* can't play, but at least I'll be there to hear *you*," Pythagoras said. "Let's go!"

At the amphitheater they waited for their turn.

"I want to stand in front," Amara said.

"But I'm shorter!" Reyna quarreled.

"Why don't you stand in a line according to height," Pythagoras said. "It should be Reyna, Amara, Thanos, Ionius, Octavius."

Pythagoras soon had the group composed. When the judges called Octavius's name, the whole group marched onto the stage.

The audience began to whisper. "Is this a joke?" "Who's going to play?" They didn't know what to think, because a group of people had never been able to play together in unison.

Pythagoras gave his cousins a nod, and they played their song. The boys piped with enthusiasm. The girls gracefully plucked their strings while standing clear of the swinging rocks. "Ode to Apollo" rang out perfectly in tune. When the song was done, there was nothing but silence.

Then everyone applauded and cheered. The lyres' rocks were still swinging when Pythagoras saw his father.

"Pythagoras," he said, "I'm surprised to see you here."

"I finished moving the rocks with my cousins' help."

"It's good that you took care of your responsibilities," replied his father. "The music sounded good, too. People are calling you the 'rock group.'"

"I like the way that sounds," Octavius said.

"This is funny," Pythagoras said to his cousins. "You're standing in the same order as when you were playing, and your heights have a similar relationship to the lengths of the pipes. So I was thinking, when we measure relationships, let's call them RATIOs for the first letters of your names."

"I'm not small now," Reyna said happily. "I'm the right size for our group."

That summer Pythagoras was better at finishing his chores. His father even gave him a new set of pipes and let him play music with his cousins every day.

Whenever they performed, they introduced themselves as Pythagoras and the Ratios—the first rock group.

Historical Note

Pythagoras (pye-THAG-uh-rus) was born on the Greek island of Samos around 569 BCE. Well known for his Pythagorean theorem, he also made important discoveries concerning musical tuning. Pythagoras discovered that notes that sound pleasant together have a particular mathematical ratio. He made a 6-note scale according to that mathematical ratio. Centuries later, musicians added more notes to get the 8-note scale that we commonly use today.

During the second century CE, Greek mathematician Nichomachus of Gerasa wrote of Pythagoras's experiment with musical strings. According to Nichomachus's story, Pythagoras hung weights from strings (similar to what young Pythagoras does in this book) and found a mathematical ratio for the harmonious sounds he created. Today's scholars point out that while the ratios as Nichomachus described them do correspond with the tones described, using weights to attain this result does not work in practice. It's likely that Pythagoras never performed this experiment, but interestingly enough, Pythagoras did successfully perform similar mathematical experiments on another stringed instrument called a monochord. Like Nichomachus's tale, our story celebrates Pythagoras's discovery of the relationship between mathematics and music.

Make an Instrument Using Pythagorean Ratios

Using six identical glasses (Pythagoras probably used thin pottery cups), put water in each glass, according to the amounts listed below. Then make up a tune by tapping the glasses with a pen.

Glass	Water	Relationship	Pythagorean ratio
6	360 ml	$\frac{360}{180}$	2 to 1
5	300 ml	$\frac{300}{180}$	5 to 3
4	270 ml	$\frac{270}{180}$	3 to 2
3	240 ml	$\frac{240}{180}$	4 to 3
2	225 ml	$\frac{225}{180}$	5 to 4
1	180 ml	$\frac{180}{180}$	1 to 1

Tuning Modern Instruments

Modern lyres don't use rocks to tune the strings. The strings are instead wrapped around pegs, which tighten or loosen the strings when turned to create tension. This is similar to how a guitar is tuned. The tension has the same effect as the weight of the rocks is meant to have for the lyres that Pythagoras tuned in this story.